T5-DHH-300

Sinners and Saints

The Insight Series

Richard G. Kapfer

CONCORDIA PUBLISHING HOUSE • SAINT LOUIS

Written by Richard G. Kapfer

Edited by Robert C. Baker

Scripture quotations are from The Holy Bible, English Standard Version®. Copyright © 2001 by Crossway Bibles, a publishing ministry of Good News Publishers, Wheaton, Illinois. Used by permission. All rights reserved.

The quotations from the Lutheran Confessions in this publication are from *Concordia. The Lutheran Confessions*, second edition, copyright © 2006 Concordia Publishing House. All rights reserved.

Hymn texts with the abbreviation *LSB* are from *Lutheran Service Book*, copyright © 2006 by Concordia Publishing House. All rights reserved.

This publication may be available in braille, in large print, or on cassette tape for the visually impaired. Please allow 8 to 12 weeks for delivery. Write to Lutheran Blind Mission, 7550 Watson Rd., St. Louis, MO 63119-4409; call toll-free 1-888-215-2455; or visit the Web site: www.blindmission.org.

Manufactured in the United States of America

1 2 3 4 5 6 7 8 9 10   16 15 14 13 12 11 10 09 08 07

Contents

Hymnal Key

LSB = Lutheran Service Book
ELH = Evangelical Lutheran Hymnary
CW = Christian Worship
LW = Lutheran Worship
LBW = Lutheran Book of Worship
TLH = The Lutheran Hymnal

About This Series

This course is one of the Insight Series of short (four-session) adult Bible study courses, each looking at an important biblical topic or theme. Using these courses, you will gain insight into a portion of the Scriptures as you hear what God is saying to you there about Himself, about yourself, and about His Good News of salvation in Jesus Christ. These insights will help you as you go about your disciple's task of living in the Word, and will equip you for a more fruitful study of the Word on your own in the future.

Using This Course

This course is designed to be used for small-group discussions. Each of the four 60- to 90-minute sessions you will find in this booklet will provide you with a clear picture of where the session is going and what it is supposed to accomplish, give you a way to lead into the session's study, provide input and discussion questions to guide your study of the text, suggest ways to follow up on the study during the week, and offer closing worship aids.

You will not need a teacher for this course. The printed material will guide you through the study. No one will have to be the answerer. But you will get the most from these materials if you:

1. Assign a leader for each session. That person should:

    a. Make sure he or she works through the material before the session and, if possible, looks at some additional resources to enrich your study.

    b. Begin and end the session with worship. The devotional time may be quite brief; a prayer or a Bible reading is sufficient. You might assign the opening and closing to a worship leader for each session.

    c. Keep the discussion moving. There is a tendency to get

bogged down on some questions or points. The leader should be willing to say, "We'd better move on to the next point."

d. Make some choices if time is limited. The leader will want to select those items from the session's content that seem to be most helpful if it is clear there will not be time to work through all of the material.

e. Listen. Make sure everyone is heard. Give each a chance to speak. Encourage participation.

f. Pray for all participants.

2. Prepare for each session. The discussion will work better, the material will be more meaningful, and the Word will speak more clearly if everyone in the class works through the session's material before the class session. Even if preparation is limited to reading through the texts that will be a part of the session's study, the effort will enrich your study.

3. Meet regularly (at least once a week) in a convenient and comfortable place. Too much time between sessions means that learning will be forgotten and much time will be used in constant review. Too little time between sessions does not allow time for you to connect what you have learned to your daily living.

4. Provide resources. Preparation that includes a chance to look at commentaries, Bible dictionaries, Bible reference books, maps, and so on will add to your class. Encourage those who do such research to contribute what they have learned or discovered as you study.

5. Encourage participation. The course offers many opportunities to discuss biblical texts and to talk about application of the Word to each individual's life. The key is sharing. Everyone should have a chance to listen and to be heard. The goal is encouragement. We want to build one another up as we study the Word. We want to share the hope and the strength we receive by the power of the Spirit through that Word. We want to allow each person to come closer to the Savior as he or she encounters Him in the Word. Emphasize the positive. Share the joy of the Gospel. Celebrate His promised presence as "two or three" gather in His name.

Participant Introduction

The session for this study booklet summarizes what Christians experience once they discover that a Christian is at one and the same time both a sinner and a saint. First there is the realization (often because of a serious sin that took us by surprise or a nagging sin that won't go away) that something is wrong. We ask: "If I'm a saint, what's wrong with me?" Then the reality hits hard that we're still sinful, and we ask, "Why don't I succeed in saintliness?" This is followed by a deeper understanding of our condition and the resulting question: "If I'm both, which one is winning?" Finally, encompassing all of our weaknesses and questions and answers is the explosion of joy: "Thank God that He's God!"

It is our hope that this course will give you insight into who you are as a sinner/saint, and that you will "thank God that He's God"!

Richard G. Kapfer

❧ Session 1 ❧

If I'm a Saint, What's Wrong with Me?

Getting Started

Read this quote from Luther as it appears in the Formula of Concord, Solid Declaration, which is one of the confessional writings of the Lutheran Church:

> O, it is a living, busy, active, mighty thing, this faith. It is impossible for it not to be doing good works incessantly. It does not ask whether good works are to be done, but before the question is asked, it has already done them, and is constantly doing them. (*Concordia: The Lutheran Confessions,* 2nd edition, p. 548)

Discuss this quote:

1. How does it describe what the Christian life ought to be?

2. In what ways does it describe your life?

3. In what ways does it make you feel inadequate? Talk about why.

Getting into the Word

The New Testament writers frequently use the word *saints* to describe Christian people. For example, as he addressed his letters to Christian congregations, Paul called the believers saints in Romans 1:7; 1 Corinthians 1:2; 2 Corinthians 1:1; Ephesians 1:1; Philippians 1:1; and Colossians 1:2. Read some of these to examine how Paul addressed these "saintly" people.

4. Would you feel comfortable if some Christian you highly respected addressed your congregation as saints? addressed your family as saints? addressed you as "St. _____" (your name)?

5a. Discuss your feelings about this. Any feelings of satisfaction?

b. Any feelings of embarrassment or even awkwardness?

Read Ephesians 2:1–7. Our saintliness is not based on mere words. It is founded on a very definite fact (v. 5). Yet without Christ, there is a definite lack of saintliness.

6. What words does the text use to describe this Christless condition?

7. When did God determine to make us "holy and blameless," that is, saints (Ephesians 1:4–5)?

8. Just how did God accomplish making us saints, according to Romans 5:6–10?

9. Discuss how Paul compares "what was" with "what is," in Romans 5:12–21.

Many blessings result from the death and resurrection of Jesus. We are no longer slaves, but free people—no longer alienated enemies of God, but reconciled friends—no longer dead, but alive!

10. Read Romans 6:5–11 and Colossians 1:21–22, and discuss what Paul means by "enslaved," "set free," "alienated," "reconciled," "dead," and "alive."

11. How saintly should you be as a saint of God? Read 1 Peter 1:14–16.

Quite a case can be made for actual, this-side-of-heaven holiness and perfection. After all, Jesus demanded it (Matthew 5:48), the Ten Commandments require it, and Christians are addressed as though they are capable of it. We can jump into almost any place in the New Testament and find this "saintly assumption."

Read Romans 12:1–2 to see this "saintly assumption" for yourself.

12a. Does this "saintly agenda" seem too aloof to you?

b. Why or why not?

Now read Romans 5:1–5. There is a purpose after all for the saintly agenda we have been given! When suffering and trouble strike us, we can still have peace with God. We know He can use it to build us up in hope.

13. Have you ever seen God using this building-up process in your life? Share it with your group.

Dealing with the Dilemma

The title of this study, "If I'm a Saint, What's Wrong with Me?" expresses the dilemma: Why don't I look like a saint? Why don't I act like one?

14. When we ignore what Scripture says and come up with our own answers, we do some strange and unsaintly things. Some of these unscriptural replies are listed below. Consider these questions for each statement: What is the real intent behind it? Why is this statement a product of human thinking, but not God's? Then jot down some notes in the spaces given, and share your findings with your group.

a. "What I did is no big deal. After all, I'm only human."

b. "But Mr. X was a well-respected member of St. Anonymous Lutheran Church! I never believed he could fall into such a terrible sin—and frankly, I'm horrified. Why, I always thought he was a Christian!"

15. You jotted down your findings; did yours agree with those of other members of your group?

16. What insights did you have to share with them?

17. What insights did they have to share with you?

18. Even more to the point, we often make "Christians will/will not" statements. Here are a few to discuss with your group. Jot down what you think of them.

a. "Christians will always tithe!"

b. "Christians will not commit adultery!"

c. "Christians will not steal!"

d. Add some other popular "Christians will/will not" statements that you have heard.

19. Now that you have added some of your own to the above list, discuss together what is basically wrong with all "Christians will/will not" statements.

Summarizing and Looking Ahead

ଔ Return to Luther's quote from the Formula of Concord at the beginning of this session. Read it together once more and then reevaluate the questions that follow it.

• Have you changed your mind about any of your answers?

• If so, how are your answers different?

ଔ Discuss the title of this chapter and share your answers to the question it asks.

ᙣ This week make a list of times and occasions when you feel "saintly." List also those times when you feel "unsaintly." Be ready to share this list. Also try to work on the question "If I'm a saint, what's wrong with me?" You may also want to begin thinking about the question implied in part of the next lesson, "If I'm a sinner, what's wrong with God?"

In Closing

Close by singing or reading in unison "Not What These Hands Have Done" (*LSB* 567; *ELH* 433; *TLH* 389).

> Not what these hands have done
> Can save this guilty soul;
> Not what this toiling flesh has borne
> Can make my spirit whole.
>
> Not what I feel or do
> Can give me peace with God;
> Not all my prayers and sighs and tears
> Can bear my awful load.
>
> Thy work alone, O Christ,
> Can ease this weight of sin;
> Thy blood alone, O Lamb of God,
> Can give me peace within.
>
> Thy love to me, O God,
> Not mine, O Lord, to Thee,
> Can rid me of this dark unrest
> And set my spirit free.
>
> Thy grace alone, O God,
> To me can pardon speak;
> Thy pow'r alone, O Son of God,
> Can this sore bondage break.

I bless the Christ of God,
    I rest on love divine,
And with unfalt'ring lip and heart
    I call this Savior mine.

Why Don't I Succeed in Saintliness?

Getting Started

Have each member of your group introduce himself or herself to the others as "St. _____" (fill in one's own name).

20a. When all introductions have been made, let each person share how the title attached to his or her name felt. Comfortable? Uncomfortable? Unrealistic? Hopeful? Joyful?

b. Explain why.

Setting Our Sights

In our last session we examined:

• our saintliness;

- how we got to be saints;

- the dilemma of our sainthood.

21. Take a few moments now to review these three points, especially if you have added a new member to your group. What Scripture reference in session 1 spoke most meaningfully to you about sainthood?

The dilemma that began to be exposed in the last session was "If I'm a saint, what's wrong with me?" In other words, we saints do not always look so saintly!

So, Who's to Blame?

There are at least two possible reasons for our lack of saintliness. There may be something wrong with me—with my willingness to obey God.

Or maybe God has failed in some way—He set the standards too high, or He failed to help me enough, so it's His fault I'm not making it!

Not surprisingly, many people conclude that either one or both of these assumptions is correct.

The trouble is, if either problem lies at the core of my failure to live as a saint, it remains up to me to "fix" things. Take a moment to discuss why this is so.

22. What possibility is there in finding peace with God—with self—under these conclusions?

Getting into the Word

Read Matthew 17:19–20. The disciples were upset because they could not cast the demon out of the boy, and they asked Jesus why they could not. Read Jesus' response for yourself. It had to do, He said, with their faith.

Many people, therefore, assume that saintliness is attainable on this side of heaven, if only they could crank themselves into getting more faith. They believe that faith is the power to accomplish anything, even perfection in themselves. They claim that if we had enough faith, we would be able to accomplish anything, to "move any mountain," such as the following:

- saving a failing marriage;

- getting that badly needed raise;

- being cured of a serious illness;

- becoming that perfect Christian spouse;

- becoming that perfect Christian parent;

- add your own!

They conclude that if we are not able to attain these desires and goals, the fault is obviously not God's but our own! Why? "Because *you lacked faith!*"

23a. Talk about these assumptions, and add any others you may have heard.

b. What kind of "faith" is meant here—faith in whom, faith in what?

24. Now look at Romans 10:17 and Ephesians 2:8–9. Where does faith come from?

It's You and Me, Lord!

The other possibility is that God didn't do everything necessary to make us saints. He did His part, and now we have to do our part.

25. If so, then grace isn't really grace. Salvation then depends partly upon God and partly upon us. Put another way, Jesus got us started, but now we have to "fill in the gaps" in order to become saintly. Call it an "It's You and me, Lord" theology. What does Paul say about this in Galatians 1:6–7?

Read Galatians 5:2–6. The apostle was attacking a group called the Judaizers, who preached that Paul took grace too far, and that Gentile Christians still had to live up to the Jewish Law (circumcision was a requirement under that Law). Perverting the Gospel of Christ is mixing Gospel with Law.

26a. How did Paul's enemies, the Judaizers, mix Gospel with Law?

b. What mixtures of Gospel and Law have you seen today?

27. Read Galatians 3:10–14. What does God say about those who want to add to what Jesus has done for our salvation?

If You Can't Reach It, Lower It

There is a third possibility! Quite popular among many people and religions (some even calling themselves Christian), this theology states: "The only way to be saintly today is to lower the standards." This belief stands on a foundation of "I'm okay, you're okay." And why? Because everything and everyone is okay.

28. People rely on the tenets of this religion all the time, primarily to avoid feelings of guilt. Discuss examples with your group. In what areas of behavior or morals have you seen changes during the past several years or decades?

29. The Bible, however, speaks very clearly about changing or lowering God's standards. What did Jesus say about this in Matthew 5:17–19?

30. Read the following, and jot down some notes. To what did Jesus refer in

a. Matthew 5:21–22?

b. Matthew 5:27–28?

c. Matthew 5:38–42?

The Dilemma

So we are called saints, but we act more like sinners. We want to do what is right and good, but we find ourselves doing what is wrong and bad. Still, we call ourselves Christians.

But are we really? Or are we just hypocrites? And if *that's* the case, perhaps there is no salvation for people like us!

31a. Read Romans 8:31–39. It's pure Gospel! It tells us that God has saved us, that God is for us, and not against us! If that is true (and God strongly assures us that it is), then why are we still such poor excuses for saints?

b. If we are sinners still (and we are), then why? Couldn't God do more?

c. Why did He allow our race to sin in the first place? Is there something wrong with God?

32. Discuss this dilemma with your group. Are there times when you wonder, "How can I be saved, but still do the things I do?" If so, that's the dilemma!—and you felt it for yourself. Share, only if you feel free to, what that dilemma is like. Do you sometimes feel like giving up? blaming God?

Dealing with the Dilemma   God's Way!

If the Bible had not met the sinner/saint dilemma head-on, it is likely that the tension of God's grace and our sin would lead every Christian into uncertainty, discouragement, and eventually despair. But God loves us too much to allow the dilemma to stand!

Read what Paul says about the dilemma of sinner/saint in Romans 7:15–23. This text may be complicated, but remember that Paul is speaking to a complicated dilemma most of us have felt. Helpful ways to approach this text are the following:

Read the text in different versions. Assuming the members of your group brought different Bible versions, have a variety of them read aloud.

33a. How are they alike?

b. How do they express the same thought differently?

c. Which version speaks most clearly to you?

34. Now put what Paul is saying into your own words. What is Paul saying about the individual who is both sinner and saint at the same time?

35. God revealed to Paul an amazing hope for all of us who are sinner/saints; state that hope in your own words.

Summarizing and Looking Ahead

ය Perhaps the thrust of this session (and the preceding one) was "old hat" for some of you. You have long been aware of the two natures warring against each other inside each Christian.

Still, we tend to overlook this sinner/saint dilemma, and often we expect both too much and too little from ourselves.

During the following week be aware of the "too much/too little" expectations you have of yourself. Note them for sharing with your group.

• If we expect too much from ourselves, are we failing to look at what God can do?

• If we expect too little, again, are we failing to see what God wants to do?

ભ Many of us may know the primary Christian teaching that salvation (being saved) is a gift of God, ours by grace through faith (Ephesians 2:8–9).

• Do we sometimes forget that living the Christian life, the life of discipleship, is also a gift from God, ours by grace through faith? Wrestle with that until your next session, and prepare to share your Bible-based conclusions with your friends.

ભ Next week we will dig into the two natures within us, as we wrestle with another question: "If I'm both (sinner/saint), which one's winning?"

In Closing

Close by singing or reading in unison "My Faith Looks Up to Thee" (*LSB* 702; *ELH* 184; *CW* 402; *LW* 378; *LBW* 479; *TLH* 394).

My faith looks up to Thee,
Thou Lamb of Calvary,
    Savior divine.
Now hear me while I pray;
Take all my guilt away;
O let me from this day
    Be wholly Thine!

May Thy rich grace impart
Strength to my fainting heart;
    My zeal inspire!
As Thou hast died for me,
Oh, may my love to Thee
Pure, warm, and changeless be,
    A living fire!

While life's dark maze I tread
And griefs around me spread,
    Be Thou my guide;
Bid darkness turn to day,
Wipe sorrow's tears away,
Nor let me ever stray
    From Thee aside.

When ends life's transient dream,
When death's cold, sullen stream
    Shall o'er me roll,
Blest Savior, then, in love,
Fear and distrust remove;
O bear me safe above,
    A ransomed soul!

❈ Session 3 ❧

If I'm Both, Which One Is Winning?

Getting Started

Share with one another your "too much/too little" expectations.

36. In what situations did you find that you were too hard on yourself?

37. In what situations did you find that you were too hard on others?

38. In what situations did you find yourself excusing your behavior or lowering your Christian standards?

Setting Our Sights

39. Read again Romans 7:15–23. Once again, put these verses into your own words.

40a. Read the following quote from the Formula of Concord, the Solid Declaration. Discuss what this means for you. Does this statement bring you any teaching from the Bible that is news to you?

b. Share what that might be.

> However, believers are not renewed in this life perfectly or completely. Their sin is covered by Christ's perfect obedience, so that it is not charged against believers for condemnation. Also, the putting to death of the old Adam [Romans 6:6] and the renewal in the spirit of their mind [Ephesians 4:23] is begun through the Holy Spirit. Nevertheless, the old Adam still clings to them in their nature and all its inward and outward powers. (*Concordia: The Lutheran Confessions,* 2nd edition, p. 559)

41. The above statement may raise some new questions for each of us. Discuss:

a. How "saintly" am I, really?

b. How "unsaintly" am I, really?

c. Which one is winning: my "new" self or my "old" self?

Getting into the Word

Read Romans 6:1–11.

42. How were you united into the death and resurrection of Christ (v. 4)?

43. What happened to our "old self" when Christ was crucified?

44a. Yet, following these words of liberation from sin, we read Paul's words in Romans 7:15–25. How can these seeming contradictions be brought together?

b. How do the words "enslaved [or "slaves"] to sin" help (Romans 6:6)?

c. How do the words "Now if I do what I do not want, it is no longer I who do it, but sin that dwells within me" help (Romans 7:20)?

45. Discuss what it means to "consider yourselves dead to sin and alive to God in Christ Jesus" (Romans 6:11). This is an invitation from God to keep our eyes on Christ Jesus, not ourselves. How does this help us in our struggle against sin?

46a. Read 1 Timothy 1:8–11. For whom is the Law of God not meant?

b. For whom is it meant?

c. In what way is the Law not meant for you?

Read Galatians 5:16–26.
47. What struggle goes on in the Christian's life?

48. Does the saintly part of you need to, or want to, respond to the Law?

49a. Discuss the following quote, and ask how it applies to you and your struggle to be the "new person" in Christ that you are. Is there a biblical teaching here that is news to you?

b. If so, what?

As far as he is a Christian or new man, he no longer needs the Law. . . . For the Christian according to his new man the Law is superfluous not merely in part, but in its every use. Without the recorded Law, the new man in him knows both what is sinful and what is good; and since the Christian is entirely godly according to the new man, he does not need the Law to keep him in check outwardly by its threats and scourges. (Francis Pieper, *Christian Dogmatics* [St. Louis, Concordia Publishing House, 1953], 3:237)

Alongside this beautiful picture of the Christian according to his or her new nature is the ugly picture of our old nature. While Paul could "delight in the law of God, in my inner being" (that is, his new nature), he also knew that "nothing good dwells in me, that is, in my flesh" (that is, his old nature). You may wish to read his words in Romans 7:22 and 18.

50a. Read Galatians 5:19–21. This is a list of the "works of the flesh." List these either on a chalkboard or on newsprint, so that your group may refer to this list.

b. What will happen to those who succumb to the works of the flesh and die to the Spirit (v. 21)?

51. Just as Paul states in Romans 7:23, there is a war going on within each of us. The question is, who's winning? Part of the answer lies in learning how tough one has to be in this war. See Colossians 3:5 and 1 Corinthians 9:26–27. What do these images tell us about the toughness of the battle?

52a. How can the knowledge that there is a battle going on within every Christian help you to understand yourself?

b. How can this knowledge help you to be more understanding of the shortcomings of others?

53. Now, how would you answer the questions posed at the beginning of this session:

a. How "saintly" am I, really?

b. How "unsaintly" am I, really?

c. Which one is winning: my "new" self or my "old" self?

Summarizing and Looking Ahead

ᘒ We Christians have within us two natures. One is perfect and holy and loves doing God's will without being told. The other is imperfect and sinful and delights in doing its own will (while rebelling against God's). What is more, the old nature isn't going to change itself or change its own mind. It can't be improved. It can only be controlled. Even then, it is still active and will be until we die.

With Paul we can say: "So I find it to be a law that when I want to do right, evil lies close at hand. For I delight in the law of God, in my inner being, but I see in my members another law waging war against the law of my mind and making me captive to the law of sin that dwells in my members. Wretched man that I am! Who will deliver me from this body of death?" (Romans 7:21–24).

But Paul does not end in despair. He adds the sentence that makes all the difference in the world: "Thanks be to God through Jesus Christ our Lord!" (Romans 7:25).

• In the meantime, keep track of moments during the week when your old nature seems to get the upper hand.

• Identify a particular situation (such as moments of envy or impatience) that triggers your old nature.

• Be prepared to share some of these thoughts in your next session.

In Closing

Close by singing or reading in unison "O Dearest Jesus, What Law Hast Thou Broken" (*LSB* 439; *ELH* 292; *CW* 117; *LW* 119; *LBW* 123; *TLH* 143).

O dearest Jesus, what law hast Thou broken
That such sharp sentence should on Thee be
    spoken?
Of what great crime hast Thou to make
    confession,
What dark transgression?

They crown Thy head with thorns, they
      smite, they scourge Thee;
With cruel mockings to the cross they urge
      Thee;
They give Thee gall to drink, they still decry
      Thee;
They crucify Thee.

Whence come these sorrows, whence this
      mortal anguish?
It is my sins for which Thou, Lord, must
      languish;
Yea, all the wrath, the woe, Thou dost
      inherit,
This I do merit.

What punishment so strange is suffered
      yonder!
The Shepherd dies for sheep that loved to
      wander;
The Master pays the debt His servants owe
      Him,
Who would not know Him.

The sinless Son of God must die in sadness;
The sinful child of man may live in gladness;
Man forfeited his life and is acquitted;
God is committed.

There was no spot in me by sin untainted;
Sick with sin's poison, all my heart had
      fainted;
My heavy guilt to hell had well-nigh brought
      me,
Such woe it wrought me.

O wondrous love, whose depth no heart hath
      sounded,
That brought Thee here, by foes and thieves
      surrounded!
All worldly pleasures, heedless, I was trying
While Thou wert dying.

O mighty King, no time can dim Thy glory!
How shall I spread abroad Thy wondrous
      story?
How shall I find some worthy gifts to proffer?
What dare I offer?

For vainly doth our human wisdom ponder—
Thy woes, Thy mercy, still transcend our
      wonder.
Oh, how should I do aught that could delight
      Thee!
Can I requite Thee?

Yet unrequited, Lord, I would not leave Thee;
I will renounce whate'er doth vex or grieve
      Thee
And quench with thoughts of Thee and
      prayers most lowly
All fires unholy.

But since my strength will nevermore suffice
      me
To crucify desires that still entice me,
To all good deeds O let Thy Spirit win me
And reign within me!

I'll think upon Thy mercy without ceasing,
That earth's vain joys to me no more be
      pleasing;
To do Thy will shall be my sole endeavor
Henceforth forever.

Whate'er of earthly good this life may grant
      me,
I'll risk for Thee; no shame, no cross, shall
      daunt me.
I shall not fear what foes can do to harm me
Nor death alarm me.

But worthless is my sacrifice, I own it;
Yet, Lord, for love's sake Thou wilt not
      disown it;
Thou wilt accept my gift in Thy great
      meekness
Nor shame my weakness.

And when, dear Lord, before Thy throne in
      heaven
To me the crown of joy at last is given,
Where sweetest hymns Thy saints forever
      raise Thee,
I, too, shall praise Thee.

Thank God That He's God!

Getting Started

In the last session we discussed the battle going on within every Christian—the "new man" against the "old man," our "saintly" self against our "unsaintly" self. We shared the frustration we often feel when the battle becomes tough and our desire to follow God's will falls far short and we do what our old nature wills. Yet we saw that we need not despair, that in Christ we will win this struggle.

Setting Our Sights

Read once again Romans 7:15–24.
54. Identify the new nature at work in these words.

55. Identify the old nature.

56. Where did our new nature come from?

57. Where did our old nature come from?

58. Why is our old nature still hanging around, causing trouble?

59. Which nature often seems to be winning, according to St. Paul? (See especially v. 24.)

In this session we will notice how Paul answers the almost panic-stricken question of verse 24 with the words, "Thanks be to God through Jesus Christ our Lord!" Although Paul does not yet explain or expand this statement of relief and joy, he does state it here as a fact. We will see why Paul thanks God through Jesus Christ.

That will be the substance of our final session: to find out why we also can thank God through Jesus for the victory He now shares with us.

Getting into the Word

Paul follows up and expands on his declaration of thanksgiving with the final words of Romans 7:25 as well as Romans 8:1–4.

Ask someone in your group to read these verses aloud, and, as a group, share what they mean. Check different Bible versions.

60. When we feel especially beaten down from guilt, as though our old nature is winning, how can God's promise in Romans 8:1 make us feel better?

In Romans 7:22–23 Paul saw two laws at war against each other, waging their battle inside of him.

61. Considering that "the law of my mind" means "the mind of Christ" (1 Corinthians 2:16; see also Romans 12:1–2), how is "the law of sin" making him a prisoner (Romans 7:23)?

We also become prisoners of "the law of sin," especially when we feel the stinging accusations of "Guilty!" from the Law. "Oh, I'll never be like Christ!" we may cry.

62a. Yet read Hebrews 4:14–16. True, we are not like Christ, but Christ Jesus became like us. Without sin, He nevertheless still felt the powerful lures of sin. What is Christ Jesus' attitude toward us now?

b. How does that help us, especially when we go to Him asking for His aid?

63. Christ Jesus will never refuse to help us. What promise in this text from Hebrews gives us every reason for confidence?

64. When guilt nags at us, and sin (especially that same old persistent sin!) haunts us again—"Oh, look at you! And you think you're a Christian?"—verse 16 tells us we can still approach the throne of grace with confidence! Share times when you have walked confidently into the throne room of your heavenly Father. How can you help friends in your Bible study group to do the same?

We learned in the last session that our old nature cannot be changed or reformed. Many church groups push reviving and reforming not only individuals, but society as well! Read the following exposition of Scripture from the Formula of Concord, Solid Declaration, and comment:

> The old Adam, like an unruly, stubborn ass, is still a part of them. It must be forced to obey Christ. It not only requires the teaching, admonition, force, and threatening of the Law, but it also often needs the club of punishments and troubles. This goes on until the body of sin is entirely put off [Romans 6:6] and a person is perfectly renewed in the resurrection. (*Concordia: The Lutheran Confessions*, 2nd edition, p. 561)

65a. Society can be changed—but is it really a change on the inside, a change of heart?

b. Why or why not?

66a. Social reform programs are necessary, of course. But do they usually come in the form of gracious invitations, or billy clubs?

b. Scripturally speaking, why are reforms so resisted?

67. What we see in society, we can often see in ourselves. Take the (uh oh!) sensitive matter of Christian giving, the use of money and other gifts from God (stewardship). What feelings does this area of discipleship to Jesus arouse in people, even the "good people" of the church?

68. When people resist faithful stewardship to Christ Jesus, it is a display of their old nature, not trusting Jesus enough to follow His direction. Yet why are Law-based stewardship pro-

grams ("Give because you should!" "Give because you ought to!") a failure, even if they appear to work on the surface?

69a. However, what is the function of the Law in stewardship?

b. But what can the Law *not* accomplish?

70a. The Gospel may seem a fragile thing upon which to base stewardship, but why is the Gospel the only way God-pleasing stewardship can happen?

b. Think of examples of both Law-oriented and Gospel-oriented stewardship ministries, and share them. What insights can you pick up of the sinner/saint at work in each?

The Formula of Concord, Solid Declaration goes on to state:

> The Law indeed says it is God's will and command that we should walk in a new life [Romans 6:4]. But it does not give the power and ability to

begin and to do it. The Holy Spirit renews the heart. He is given and received, not through the Law, but through the preaching of the Gospel (Galatians 3:14). (*Concordia: The Lutheran Confessions*, 2nd edition, p. 559)

71. Whether in the matter of our stewardship to Christ, or in some other area of discipleship or willing obedience to God, what is the Law completely unable to do?

Evaluate your own stewardship, evangelism/witnessing, support of missions, support of recruiting young people for pastoral or teaching ministries:

72. If you have been driven by the Law, any support of these may have been begrudged—a have-to rather than get-to spirit. However, how does the Holy Spirit invite and upbuild us through the Gospel?

73. List some specific servanthood opportunities you see that the "saintly" you (who draws on the power of the Gospel) can embrace within your congregation.

This raises the question of how the "new you" (you, the redeemed saint, the "new man") is nurtured. Read Jesus' words on this in John 15:1–8, 13–15.

Remaining in Jesus entails remaining in His Word; and He remains in us. This becomes very practical! For when the old man, the flesh, rises up in civil war against the new man Christ put in us, there is a way we can win!

74. Rather than to look introspectively at ourselves ("Oh, how am I doing as a new-man-Christian?") and become disheartened, we are instead invited to look at Jesus. Read for yourself what He said in verse 13. How does it feel to be loved that much?

75. Jesus honors us more than we'd dare ask. Servants are not let in on the Master's plans, but we are! Instead of calling us servants, what does Jesus call us (vv. 13–15)?

Remaining in Jesus entails remaining in His Word; and He remains in us. Read 1 Corinthians 10:16–17.

76a. How does faith come in the first place?

b. How does it, then, grow?

77. The Word, proclaimed from Scripture or administered in the Sacraments, is God's way of keeping His saints forgiven, nourished, and refreshed. How do you respond to Christ's invitation to be nourished by Word and Sacrament?

In Conclusion

ଔ Christians can unashamedly proclaim that they are saints! There is always a struggle (on this side of heaven), and that is why both the Law and the Gospel are absolutely vital. Both keep the struggle alive!

• As disheartened as we may become that there still is a struggle between our old and new natures, what does the fact that there is a struggle show us?

ଔ Christians, therefore, do not press on toward a hoped-for victory. We press on from the victory Jesus won on His cross!

• How does that Good News encourage us in our day-to-day struggles as His saints?

• How can we help each other, in some practical way, to share that victory even if we do not yet see it completely?

ଔ Before you leave this session, be sure to have a prayer. Thank God that He has worked out a way to call sinners "saints"; thank Christ Jesus that He calls us "friends"; thank the Holy Spirit for the way He nourishes us with Word and Sacrament.

In other words, thank God that He's God!

In Closing

Close by singing or reading in unison "Salvation unto Us Has Come" (*LSB* 555; *ELH* 227; *CW* 390; *LW* 355; *LBW* 297; *TLH* 377).

Salvation unto us has come
    By God's free grace and favor;
Good works cannot avert our doom,
    They help and save us never.
Faith looks to Jesus Christ alone,
Who did for all the world atone;
    He is our one Redeemer.

What God did in His Law demand
    And none to Him could render
Caused wrath and woe on ev'ry hand
    For man, the vile offender.
Our flesh has not those pure desires
The spirit of the Law requires,
    And lost is our condition.

It was a false, misleading dream
    That God His Law had given
That sinners could themselves redeem
    And by their works gain heaven.
The Law is but a mirror bright
To bring the inbred sin to light
    That lurks within our nature.

From sin our flesh could not abstain,
    Sin held its sway unceasing;
The task was useless and in vain,
    Our guilt was e'er increasing.
None can remove sin's poisoned dart
Or purify our guileful heart—
    So deep is our corruption.

Yet as the Law must be fulfilled
     Or we must die despairing,
Christ came and has God's anger stilled,
     Our human nature sharing.
He has for us the Law obeyed
And thus the Father's vengeance stayed
     Which over us impended.

Since Christ has full atonement made
     And brought to us salvation,
Each Christian therefore may be glad
     And build on this foundation.
Your grace alone, dear Lord, I plead,
Your death is now my life indeed,
     For You have paid my ransom.

Let me not doubt, but truly see
     Your Word cannot be broken;
Your call rings out, "Come unto Me!"
     No falsehood have You spoken.
Baptized into Your precious name,
My faith cannot be put to shame,
     And I shall never perish.

The Law reveals the guilt of sin
     And makes us conscience-stricken;
But then the Gospel enters in
     The sinful soul to quicken.
Come to the cross, trust Christ, and live;
The Law no peace can ever give,
     No comfort and no blessing.

Faith clings to Jesus' cross alone
     And rests in Him unceasing;
And by its fruits true faith is known,
     With love and hope increasing.
For faith alone can justify;
Works serve our neighbor and supply
     The proof that faith is living.

All blessing, honor, thanks, and praise
    To Father, Son, and Spirit,
The God who saved us by His grace;
    All glory to His merit.
O triune God in heav'n above,
You have revealed Your saving love;
    Your blessed name we hallow.